THE
SUPER BOWL

by
Jane Duden

CRESTWOOD HOUSE
New York

Maxwell Macmillan Canada
Toronto

Maxwell Macmillan International
New York Oxford Singapore Sydney

Library of Congress Cataloging-in-Publication Data
Duden, Jane
  The Super Bowl / by Jane Duden.
    p. cm. — (Sportslines)
    Summary: Examines the history, significant plays and players, and other memorable
moments of the Super Bowl.
  ISBN 0-89686-725-0
    1. Super Bowl Game (Football)—Juvenile literature. |1. Super Bowl Game (Football)—
History. 2. Football—History.| I. Title. II. Series.
  GV956.2.S8D83   1992
  796.332'648—dc20   91-24692

Photo Credits
All photos courtesy of AP—Wide World Photos

Macmillan Publishing Company   Maxwell Macmillan Canada, Inc.
866 Third Avenue   1200 Eglinton Avenue East
New York, NY 10022   Suite 200
                                Don Mills, Ontario M3C 3N1

CRESTWOOD HOUSE

Macmillan Publishing Company is part of the Maxwell Communication Group of Companies.

Produced by Flying Fish Studio

Printed in the United States of America

First edition

10 9 8 7 6 5 4 3 2 1

Contents

The Vince Lombardi Trophy

Introduction

Each January the two best teams in pro football battle for the NFL (National Football League) crown and the Vince Lombardi Trophy. Since 1967 the NFL championship has been decided at the Super Bowl. Find out how today's modern NFL and the Super Bowl got started. Read about the powerhouse teams that clashed in the Super Bowl. Meet the great plays and players. Get the inside stories on exciting comebacks, big upsets, and wild moments. The Super Bowl has had them all!

The Football Money Wars

When the American Football League (AFL) was formed in 1959, many NFL officials were upset. They were the pioneers. They'd been around since 1920. Thanks to the NFL, football had become a major American sport. The NFL resented the new league. They felt the newcomer would not last. But the players felt differently. They liked the new AFL. Why? Their salaries soared as the two leagues tried to outbid each other for the best football players. The "money wars" led to a bitter rivalry between the NFL and the AFL. If the money wars kept on, both leagues would go broke.

A Merger Cools the Rivalry

In 1966 the NFL and the AFL agreed to join together. The move ended the costly competition between the leagues. It provided for a common draft of college players in 1967. The merger formed today's National Football League. The new NFL had two conferences. The old NFL was renamed the National Football Conference (NFC). A second conference was formed. It was named the American Football Conference (AFC). At the end of each season, the champions of the two conferences would play each other in a championship game.

The leagues knew they couldn't complete the details of the merger until 1970. But they agreed to play the "AFL-NFL World Championship Game" right away. The first title game would be played at the end of the 1966 season. Each league would play its regular schedule for the season. Each would come up with a champion of its own. Then the two champions would meet on the second Sunday in January in 1967. The winning team would become the best overall team for that season.

The Name of the Game

The name of the Super Bowl came by accident. One evening in 1966, Lamar Hunt came home to find his daughter playing with a super-bouncy ball. She told him it was called a super ball. Mr. Hunt was the owner of the AFL's Kansas City Chiefs. He had the AFL-NFL championship game on his mind. The official name—AFL-NFL World Championship Game—was long and awkward. From his daughter's comment, Hunt created the name Super Bowl. The name stuck. Each year the Super Bowl is further identified by the addition of a Roman numeral.

1967 Super Bowl I: The First Historic Game

Super Bowl I was played at the Los Angeles Memorial Coliseum. The date was January 15, 1967. The NFL champion was the powerhouse Green Bay Packers. Vince Lombardi was their crusty coach. The Packers faced the upstarts of the AFL, the Kansas City Chiefs. Most fans felt that *no* team in the infant AFL could handle the rugged NFL teams. But the Chiefs put up a good fight. The game was a close 14-10 at the half. Then the Packers took control. Kansas City fought back, but the experience of the veterans was paying off. Kansas City's superdream came to a nightmare end. Packers quarterback Bart Starr completed 16 of 23 passes for 250 yards. The Packers crushed the Chiefs 35-10.

Some fans said Super Bowl I proved the young AFL couldn't handle an NFL team. Others argued that hardly any team in *either* league was strong enough to hold up to the Packers for a full 60 minutes. Even Coach Lombardi made light of the Super Bowl. He said in order to be a great game, it had to have tradition.

1968 Super Bowl II: Another Win for the NFL

Super Bowl II was played on January 14, 1968, at Miami's Orange Bowl. The NFL's Green Bay Packers were back. They played the Oakland Raiders, champs of the AFL. Super Bowl II ended 33-14 in favor of the Packers. Again the veteran Packers were the best in the nation. Both Super Bowl triumphs had been solid ones for the NFL. Many people felt that the Super Bowl battles might as well stop. Maybe the AFL teams just weren't strong enough for the competition.

A victorious Vince Lombardi at Super Bowl II, his final game as coach

Super Bowl II was the final game for Vincent Lombardi. The Packers' leader was retiring as coach. He had a new job with Green Bay's front office. His team had given him a wonderful victory for his final game.

The Prizes

What are the stakes for the Super Bowl? The winning team gets the Vince Lombardi Trophy. The 21-inch sterling-silver trophy was named for the legendary coach of the Green Bay Packers. Lombardi was famous for his dedication to winning. He said: "Winning isn't everything. It's the only thing."

Players on the winning team each receive a ring and a cash prize.

Broadway Joe and the AFL

The AFL would have to prove itself in Super Bowl III. The AFL had been formed by a group of young businessmen. They had energy and money. They worked hard to make the league survive. During the bidding wars before the merger, the New York Jets had offered Joe Namath the largest contract ever given a pro football player up to that time. The president of the Jets was Sonny Werblin. He knew he needed to build his franchise with somebody who could do more than just play football. He was looking for a good passer with a personality. He saw what he wanted in Joe Namath. Joe loved flashy living, parties, and money. He also loved football. He joined the Jets and moved to New York. Joe's courage and talent on the football field gave the AFL respectability. His flashy life-style gave Namath the name Broadway Joe. Joe was angered by the claims that AFL teams were too weak to compete with the NFL. Super Bowl III was coming up. Many were sure that nothing would change and the NFL would win. The Jets were 18-point underdogs. Joe Namath didn't buy those odds. He made headlines all over the nation by saying so. Joe stood up at a public awards dinner the week before the game and said: "The Jets will win Sunday. I guarantee it." His promise made big headlines.

1969 Super Bowl III: What Joe Promises, Joe Delivers

Super Bowl III was a battle between the AFL's New York Jets and the NFL's Baltimore Colts. The game was played in Miami on January 12, 1969. Baltimore was led by their veteran quarterback, Johnny Unitas. The Jets were led by Joe Namath. On Super Sunday, Namath's talent proved to be as big as his boasts. During the first quarter the Jets proved they could play with the Colts. Baltimore missed a chance to score. With each play, the Jets offense grew more confident. Before long, Jets fullback Matt Snell was ripping off big gains, even hurting people as he ran. Namath began mixing his plays. He threw to his backs and his wide receivers. He was backing up his boast with his quick arm and sharp mind. The Jets made the game's first score. At halftime, it was still a 7-0 game. The final score was Jets 16, Colts 7. It wasn't a gigantic score, but the Jets had dominated the entire game. What Joe promised, Joe delivered. No doubt about it, the American Football League had arrived. What's more, the Jets' accomplishment made the Super Bowl *super*. It was the biggest upset in the short history of the Super Bowl. Now the game had tradition!

Joe Namath delivers at Super Bowl III!

Where's the Trophy?

Every pro football team dreams of bringing home the Vince Lombardi Trophy. Now the underdog Jets had won the grand prize! But when the Jets left Miami, they forgot the very thing they had worked so hard to get. On the flight home, they asked one another: "Where is the trophy? Who has the trophy?" The Jets had nothing to show the mob of fans waiting for them in New York. Someone found the trophy back at the team's Florida hotel, next to some left-behind equipment.

1970 Super Bowl IV: The End of an Era

Super Bowl IV was the end of an era. The AFL was closing shop. Its merger with the NFL was complete. Super Bowl IV would be the last real battle between the old leagues. It took place in New Orleans on January 11, 1970. The Kansas City Chiefs (AFL) met the Minnesota Vikings (NFL). The Vikings were 14-point favorites.

When the Chiefs arrived at Tulane Stadium, they found a surprise. A patch that read AFL 10 was sewn to each uniform. It stood for the AFL's 10-year history. Hank Stram coached the Chiefs that day. He said: "We were the second-winningest team in the history of the AFL, and we were proud of it. Those patches made us even more determined to go out with a bang."

They did. Kansas City beat the Minnesota Vikings 23-7. It was one of the biggest upsets in Super Bowl history. The Chiefs held the Minnesota offense to just two first downs. Their kicker, Jan Stenerud, kicked the longest field goal ever seen in Super Bowl play—48 yards! He kicked two more

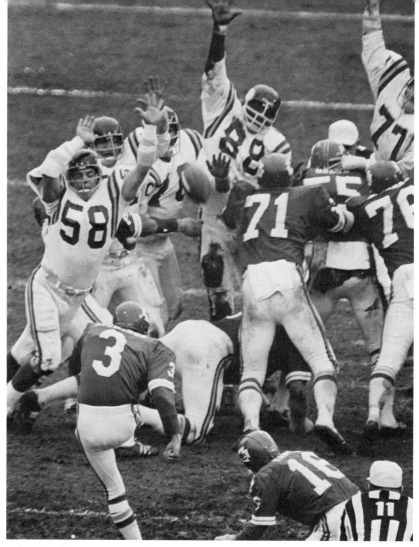

The Chiefs' Jan Stenerud kicks the ball toward the goal posts.

successful field goals before the day was done. Kansas City more than made up for their loss to the Packers in Super Bowl I. For a second time, an AFL team had taken the championship.

The Modern NFL

In 1970 the AFL-NFL merger was completed. The *new* National Football League came into being. The AFL joined it as the American Football Conference. The old NFL became the National Football Conference. The Baltimore Colts, Cleveland Browns, and Pittsburgh Steelers were moved from the old NFL to the new AFL. Each conference then had 13 teams. Each conference was split into three divisions. The new NFL looked like this:

NFC	AFC
Eastern Division	*Eastern Division*
Dallas Cowboys	Baltimore Colts
New York Giants	Boston Patriots
Philadelphia Eagles	Buffalo Bills
St. Louis Cardinals	Miami Dolphins
Washington Redskins	New York Jets
Central Division	*Central Division*
Chicago Bears	Cincinnati Bengals
Detroit Lions	Cleveland Browns
Green Bay Packers	Houston Oilers
Minnesota Vikings	Pittsburgh Steelers
Western Division	*Western Division*
Atlanta Falcons	Denver Broncos
New Orleans Saints	Kansas City Chiefs
Los Angeles Rams	Oakland Raiders
San Francisco 49ers	San Diego Chargers

A system of playoffs was devised to produce a champion for each conference. The playoffs would include a "wild card" team from each conference. (The wild card is the team with the next best record.) In the first year of the new NFL, the top teams in the NFC divisions were the Cowboys, Vikings, and 49ers. The Lions got the wild card playoff spot. The AFC divisional winners were Baltimore, Cincinnati, and Oakland. Miami went into the postseason as a wild card. After the playoffs, the Cowboys and the Colts were the two conference winners. They headed for Miami's Orange Bowl and Super Bowl V.

1971 Super Bowl V: The Blooper Bowl

Super Bowl V was played January 17, 1971, in front of 80,055 screaming fans. It had everything—strange plays, a nail-biting finish, and so many mistakes that the sportswriters called it the Blooper Bowl. The excitement began right away. Colts quarterback Johnny Unitas tried a pass. It was intercepted by Cowboy linebacker Chuck Howley. Next, Cowboy quarterback Craig Morton fired the ball far above his leaping receiver, blowing a chance for a touchdown. Later, Craig passed to an ineligible receiver. Again, the Cowboys missed a touchdown chance. Dallas was one blooper ahead. Then Baltimore turned their next goof into a score. The pass was fumbled among three Colts' players before ending in a touchdown! Then Johnny Unitas fumbled and opened the way for a Dallas score. The Cowboys moved ahead 13-6. Not long after, Unitas left the game with injured ribs. In the third quarter Dallas missed a touchdown for the third time. Now Earl

14

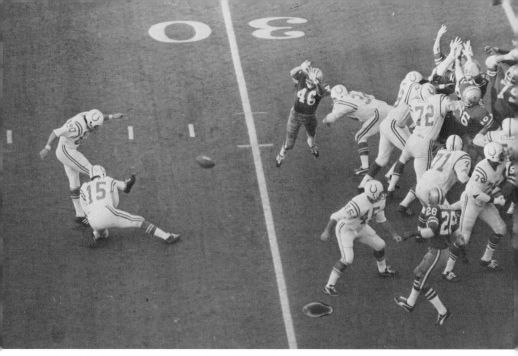

The Colts' Jim O'Brien wins the "Blooper" Bowl.

Morrall was in for the injured Unitas. He led the way deep into Dallas territory. Then he fired a good pass, but Dallas's Chuck Howley intercepted—again! There were more mistakes to come. Finally with 7:35 left to play, the score stood tied at 13-13. The clock ticked down to 1:09 with the score still tied. The game got a hair-raising finish when the Colts ran the clock down to 9 seconds. They brought in rookie kicker Jim O'Brien for a 32-yard field goal try. If he missed, the game would go into overtime. The kick was good! The score was Colts 16, Cowboys 13. Baltimore won the wildest Super Bowl ever. And they won the first Super Bowl between two teams from the old NFL.

MVP of the Blooper Bowl

Chuck Howley, Dallas linebacker, was in the locker room with the rest of his gloomy teammates. They had just lost Super Bowl V. Then someone broke the glum silence. It was announced that Chuck Howley had won the MVP (Most Valuable Player) award! It was the only time in Super Bowl history that a member of the losing team was named MVP. Chuck won the honor for a fumble recovery and two interceptions. A week later, he went to New York and accepted his prizes—a trophy and a car. He still has the trophy. The car was another story. "It was too hot for me. My wife drove it for six months. Then we traded it in for a station wagon."

1972 Super Bowl VI: Another Great Moment for Howley

It was January 16, 1972. Chuck Howley and the Dallas Cowboys (NFC) were in New Orleans for Super Bowl VI. They played the Miami Dolphins (AFC). Chuck Howley had another great moment in his career in the fourth quarter. Miami was trailing 17-3. Howley intercepted and covered 41 yards before he was hit at the Dolphin nine. His play set up the final tally for the day. Mike Ditka scored on a pass from Roger Staubach, giving Dallas a 24-3 win over Miami. Miami's 3 points were the least ever posted in Super Bowl battles. As for the Cowboys, they won their first Super Bowl! This time Chuck Howley got a ring. He still has it.

Roger Staubach tries to escape the grasp of Miami Dolphins defender Jim Riley.

1973 Super Bowl VII: The Dolphin's Perfect Season

In Super Bowl VII, the Miami Dolphins were ready for revenge. They had gone undefeated in the regular season. The Dolphins had an accurate passer in quarterback Bob Griese. They had a rhino of a runner in a fullback named Larry Csonka. (Some sportswriters compared the 6'3", 235-pound Csonka to a rhinoceros.) And they had a tough, tight, daring defense. The combination was unbeatable.

The Dolphins showed they were the biggest fish in the pro football pond. They had no trouble beating the Washington Redskins 14-7. Washington was able to score only once. It came in the fourth quarter on a freakish play. Gary Yepremian's field goal attempt for Miami was blocked. When Gary picked up the ball and tried to pass, it floated into the hands of Redskin Mike Bass. Bass ran with it 49 yards for a Redskins touchdown! The funny play made headlines everywhere. But that was all for Washington. It was Miami's 17th game—and 17th win. They were the first team in the new National Football League to play a perfect season. And they were in for more glory ahead.

1974 Super Bowl VIII: Dolphins Again

The Miami Dolphins were back again! Only four years ago Miami had been a losing team. Don Shula took over as coach. Now the Dolphins were the first team ever to compete in three Super Bowls. And they had a chance to match Green Bay's record of back-to-back wins. The Dolphins were going against Coach Bud Grant's Minnesota Vikings.

Larry Csonka smashes through a tackle.

The Vikings had Fran Tarkenton, one of the best quarter-backs in pro football. And they had a top-notch defense nicknamed "the Purple People Eaters." It promised to be anybody's game. The Dolphins and the Vikings both had 12-2 records for the 1973 season. Both had beat tough teams to win their conference championship. And both had won their conference championship by the identical score: 27-10!

19

Miami totally dominated the game. Two drives in the first quarter resulted in touchdowns by Larry Csonka and Jim Kiick. Gary Yepremian added a field goal in the second period. The score at the half was 17-0. In the third quarter the Dolphins marched again. Csonka scored another touchdown. The Vikings' Fran Tarkenton was not about to see his team shamed by a scoreless day. They got on the scoreboard in the last period when Fran Tarkenton kept the ball on a running play and scored a touchdown. The final score was 24-7.

Records in Super Bowl VIII

Coach Don Shula matched Vince Lombardi's record for Super Bowl wins. His team became the first since Green Bay in Super Bowls I and II to win the classic two years straight. Of all the NFL teams, only Shula's Dolphins had been to three Super Bowls. Miami's Larry Csonka posted 145 yards on 33 carries. The old record belonged to Matt Snell of the Jets. He had posted 121 yards in Super Bowl III. These were great records. But they would soon be broken. The winning years of the Pittsburgh Steelers were about to dawn!

1975 Super Bowl IX: It's Been a Long Time Coming!

If there was a tough, gritty team in the 1970s, it was the Pittsburgh Steelers. After 42 hungry, losing years, the Pittsburgh Steelers had won a championship. They were going to their first Super Bowl.

In Super Bowl IX, Pittsburgh met the Minnesota Vikings. If the Steelers were hungry for a title, the Vikings were starving. Minnesota had already played in two Super Bowls but lost both times. Would the third time be the lucky charm? They had many things in their favor. The Vikes had versatile halfback Chuck Foreman. They had scrambling quarterback Fran Tarkenton. And they had a defense equal to that of the Steelers' "Steel Curtain."

It was a game of awesome defenses. Minnesota's only score came in the fourth period. They scored on a blocked punt that was recovered in the end zone. The extra point was missed. The score was Steelers 9, Vikings 6. Then Steelers quarterback Terry Bradshaw engineered a seven minute drive that ended in a touchdown. The game ended at 16-6. The Steelers were world champions at last!

1976 Super Bowl X: The Best Battle Ever

In 1976 the Dallas Cowboys became the first wild card team to reach the Super Bowl. After a 10-4 season, the Cowboys walloped the Los Angeles Rams 37-7 to win the

Pittsburgh Steelers' Lynn Swann dives to complete a pass.

conference crown. Dallas faced the Pittsburgh Steelers, back for the second year in a row. The Steelers had a 12-2 record in the AFC for the 1975 season.

Many sportswriters felt it was one of the best championship battles ever. And most agree, this game belonged to the Steeler's Lynn Swann. Pittsburgh's wide receiver put on one of the greatest shows in Super Bowl history. He caught just four passes, but they were good for 161 yards. Three of them had been the most spectacular catches ever seen in Super Bowl play. The fourth was a blazing touchdown that earned Swann Most Valuable Player honors. And Swann hadn't been sure he would play at all. He had suffered a concussion in the AFC title match against Oakland. It wasn't decided that he would play until just minutes before the kickoff. The Steelers won the championship, 21-17.

1977 Super Bowl XI: Minnesota Vikings Try Again

Many thought it was about time for Bud Grant and his Minnesota Vikings to win the Super Bowl. This was Minnesota's fourth trip. John Madden and his Oakland Raiders did not agree. In the late 1960s and early 1970s, the Oakland Raiders were the winningest team in professional football. But they failed to become Super Bowl champions until 1977.

After a scoreless first period, Oakland took control of the game and never let loose of it. Oakland had a 16-0 lead at the half. The Vikings finally scored in the third period. But the Raiders won the game 32-14. It made up for the 33-14 beating they had taken from Green Bay in Super Bowl II.

Oakland Raider Ken Stabler gains 17 yards.

Records in Super Bowl XI

The game brought 100,421 fans to the Pasadena Rose Bowl on January 9, 1977, for a record crowd. Next, Oakland set a rushing record of 266 yards on the ground. The old record belonged to the Dallas Cowboys. They had rushed for 252 yards in Super Bowl VI. Minnesota set an unhappy record. They had played in more Super Bowl games than any other team—four. They hadn't won a single one.

23

A happy Roger Staubach after completing a long touchdown

1978 Super Bowl XII: First Indoor Game

Super Bowl XII was the first championship battle to take place indoors. It was played at the New Orleans Superdome on January 15, 1978. Tom Landry's Cowboys were back for their fourth Super Bowl. The Denver Broncos were never really in the game. The Cowboys were ahead 13-0 at the half. Denver got its lone touchdown on a one-yard plunge by Rob Lytle. The best moments came in the fourth quarter. Cowboy running back Robert Newhouse had the ball. He saw wide receiver Golden Richards in the end zone as the Broncos charged in on him. Newhouse lofted a 29-yard pass to Richards. Richards grabbed it with an over-the-head catch for a touchdown. The final score was 27-10, Cowboys. In four trips to the Super Bowl, the Cowboys had won two, lost two.

Records in Super Bowl XII

Some sportswriters called Super Bowl XII the poorest one ever played. It had the most fumbles in Super Bowl history, with ten in all. It also produced the most penalties, 20. Dallas had 12 penalties for 94 yards. Denver lost 60 yards on 8 penalties.

24

1979 Super Bowl XIII: The Steelers Make It Three

The Steelers had won two Super Bowls in a row. The Green Bay Packers had also won two in a row. The Miami Dolphins had won two in a row just before the Steelers. But no team had yet won three in a row.

In 1979 the Steelers were back hoping for their third win. Waiting for them were their old foes from Super Bowl X and the defending champions—the Dallas Cowboys. The Cowboys were the first team to appear in five Super Bowls. Thirteen is supposed to be an unlucky number. But Super Bowl XIII was an absolutely super Super Bowl, the highest scoring in all history. When the two champions got together on January 21, 1979, they set a new record. The score was up to 35-31, the highest ever seen in Super Bowl play.

Super Bowl XIII, a lucky number for the winning Pittsburgh Steelers

The game was a thriller from start to finish. Terry Bradshaw fired a 28-yard TD pass to John Stallworth in the first quarter to give the Steelers an early lead. Then the Cowboys did what no other team had done all season long. They scored against the Steelers in the first period. The game was a 7-7 deadlock after one quarter. Then Dallas burst into the lead, 14-7. Bradshaw flipped a short pass to Stallworth. Stallworth turned a 10-yard pass into a 75-yard scoring play—a new record. The extra point was good. The score was tied up at 14-14. Then Pittsburgh's Rocky Bleier scored on a short pass from Bradshaw. The score at the half was 21-14, Pittsburgh. The only score in the third period was a 27-yard Dallas field goal. Then Pittsburgh took hold. Franco Harris scored on a 22-yard run. Lynn Swann took an 18-yard touchdown pass from Bradshaw. The score was now 35-17. Pittsburgh's lead seemed impossible to overcome. But Dallas's Staubach wasn't finished. He engineered a drive from his own 11 to the Steeler 7. Tony Dorsett gave a 29-yard dash. Then Staubach passed a touchdown shot to tight end Billy Joe Dupree. With the extra point, the score was now Pittsburgh 35, Dallas 24. The game was in its final minutes. Dallas needed a fast 11 points. Then Staubach threw another touchdown pass to Butch Johnson after recovering an onsides kick. The crowd could not believe what it was seeing. The score was now 35-31. There were only 22 seconds remaining. Dallas had come close to a miracle comeback. But the clock ran out. Pittsburgh won, 35-31.

The Steelers had won a record-setting third Super Bowl. Terry Bradshaw was the MVP with a 318-yard, four touchdown game.

1980 Super Bowl XIV: Steelers Ram the Rams

The Steelers were *the* team of the seventies, just as the Green Bay Packers had been the team of the sixties. They finished the 1979 season 12-4, with another AFC Central crown. In 1980 the Steelers were back at the Super Bowl for a fourth time. They had the same veterans that had been in the three previous Super Bowl triumphs: Quarterback Terry Bradshaw; running backs Franco Harris and Rocky Bleier; receivers Lynn Swann and John Stallworth. In the defense line was "Mean" Joe Greene, L. C. Greenwood, Dwight White, and Ernie Holmes. Jack Ham, Jack Lambert, and Andy Russell were linebackers. The hard-hitting Mel Blount and Donnie Shell were a strong secondary. The Steelers went to work against the Los Angeles Rams.

Quarterback Terry Bradshaw leads the Pittsburgh Steelers to their fourth Super Bowl win.

The Rams weren't easy. The Rams led 7-3 after one quarter, 13-10 at the half, and 19-17 after three quarters. But the tide turned with Bradshaw's passing and the Steel Curtain's defense. The Steelers decided to go for broke. They tried a play they had practiced all week with only one success. It worked—for a 73-yard touchdown play! The fans were wide-eyed. The kick made it a 24-19 game. Then Franco Harris smashed over for the touchdown that won the game. The Curtain held back the Rams. The final score was Steelers 31, Rams 19.

Super Bowl XIV Records

The fans set the first, with a record attendance of 103,985. The Steelers set the second. The Pittsburgh Steelers had played in four Super Bowls. They had won them all. They were the winningest team in Super Bowl history!

1981 Super Bowl XV: A Raid on the Eagles

The Raiders faced the Eagles at the Superdome in New Orleans on January 25, 1981. This was the first Super Bowl for Coach Dick Vermeil's Eagles. For the Raiders, it was the third. Their quarterback, Jim Plunkett, had been called "washed up." But Jim had led the Raiders to the wild card spot in the playoffs. Oakland became the first wild card team in the AFC to go all the way to the Super Bowl. Plunkett's teammates had promised to give their quarterback plenty of protection in Super Bowl XV. They did, and he proved his career was far from over.

The Raiders also had a linebacker named Rod Martin. Coaches had said Rod was too small, at 6'2" and 215 pounds,

Jim Plunkett's pass gains 80 yards for the Oakland Raiders.

to play his position. But Rod led all the Oakland linebackers in tackles during the 1980 season. In Super Bowl XV, he drove Philadelphia crazy with his interceptions.

The Raiders surged to a 14-0 lead in the first quarter. One of the plays had netted 80 yards! It was Jim Plunkett's pass to Kenny King. It still stands as the longest scoring play in Super Bowl history! At halftime, the score was 14-3. It reached 21-3 in the third quarter. Then Rod Martin starred again with his second interception. Oakland called on Chris Bahr for a field goal. Chris kicked a 46-yarder. Oakland's lead went to 24-3. There was more to come for Rod. His third interception was a Super Bowl record. The linebacker threaded his way to gain 25 yards. His teammates swamped him with cheers and slaps. It was too late for Philadelphia. Super Bowl XV ended with the score 27-10.

1982 Super Bowl XVI: San Francisco 49ers vs. Cincinnati Bengals

The 1982 Super Bowl was played at the Silverdome in Pontiac, Michigan. The San Francisco 49ers won their first Super Bowl, downing the Cincinnati Bengals. Joe Montana guided a drive for San Francisco in the first quarter. It ended in a touchdown he made himself. By the half, the 49ers had another touchdown and a pair of field goals. The score was 20-0, San Francisco. The Bengals came back in the second half. Quarterback Ken Anderson made Cincinnati's first score. He later drilled a pass to Dan Ross for another touchdown. But the 49ers defense made the day for San Francisco. They defeated the Bengals 26-21.

Joe Montana sneaks a touchdown.

1983 Super Bowl XVII: Washington Redskins vs. Miami Dolphins

Don Shula was back with his Miami Dolphins. The Washington Redskins weren't impressed with past records. They were there to prove they were champions. The two teams met at the Rose Bowl in Pasadena on January 30, 1983.

It looked like Miami might give Shula his third Super Bowl trophy. The Dolphins' Fulton Walker gave the crowd a dazzler. Walker ran the kickoff back 98 yards for a touchdown to give the Dolphins a 17-10 lead at the half. But the Redskins' coach, Joe Gibbs, got his team fired up for the second half. The Redskins came back out and totally shut down Miami. The Skins scored on a field goal by Mark Moseley. They scored on a 43-yard run by John Riggins. They scored on a short pass from Joe Theismann to Charlie Brown. It was a win for Washington, 27-17.

A Colorful Character for Super Bowl XVII

Only nine regular season games were played in 1982. It was a strike year for the NFL Players Union. Replacement players filled in until the strike ended. Fans were angry. Then John Riggins lightened things up. Riggins was a player for the Washington Redskins. He was a colorful character. He held a press conference wearing battle fatigues. People forgot the bad stuff. Super Bowl XVII became a John Riggins event. It was a game between the Hogs (Washington offensive line) and Killer Bees (Miami defense). After the opening kickoff, Riggins gained 116 yards. He increased his carries with each quarter. His highlight came in the final period, fourth-and-one at the Miami 43. Riggins burst through the line. He shook off cornerback Don McNeal and ran all the way to the end zone. The final score was Washington 27, Miami 17. Riggins declared: "Reagan may be president, but I'm the king!"

1984 Super Bowl XVIII: Los Angeles Raids Redskins

The Raiders had moved from Oakland to Los Angeles. They came to Tampa Stadium in 1984 as the Los Angeles Raiders. The Redskins were back to win their second-in-a-row Super Bowl. But everything went wrong for Washington from the start. The Raiders scored first. By halftime, they had a 21-3 lead. The Redskins scored in the second half, but from that point on it was all Los Angeles. First a 5-yard TD jaunt by Marcus Allen. Then he took off around end and went 74 yards for the clinching touchdown. Chris Bahr's final field goal topped it off. The Raiders triumphed, 38-9.

Marcus Allen was named MVP. Allen had the greatest game of his career in XVIII. He rushed for 191 yards and two touchdowns.

1985 Super Bowl XIX: Lopsided Battle of the Quarterbacks

Super Bowl XIX was January 20, 1985, at Stanford Stadium in Palo Alto, CA. The Miami Dolphins met the San Francisco 49ers. The game was billed as the battle of the quarterbacks. The QBs were San Francisco's Joe Montana and Miami's Dan Marino. Montana had wiped out NFL passing records since he joined the 49ers in 1979. But the big battle turned out to be one-sided.

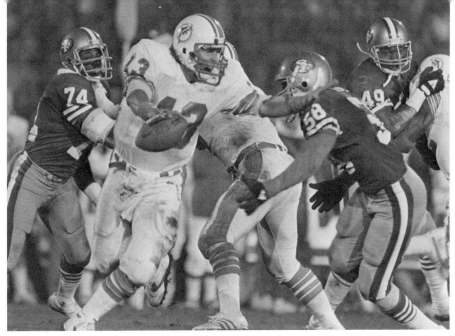
Super Bowl XIX, the Battle of the Quarterbacks

The Dolphins were in the game for the first quarter. Uwe von Schamann kicked a field goal for the Dolphins early. Then Montana threw a TD strike to Carl Monroe for the 49ers. Miami's Marino came right back. He zinged one to Dan Johnson to regain the lead. But then the red-hot 49ers took apart the Miami defense. They did it by taking the Dolphins out of their scheme and forcing Marino to play from behind. Montana hit Roger Craig for a touchdown. Then each of those two in turn ran the ball in for touchdowns. For Miami, von Schamann booted a pair of field goals. The score at half was San Francisco 28, Dolphins 16. The Frisco defense did it all in the second half. They shut out Miami while Ray Wersching kicked a field goal. Montana and Craig again teamed up on a touchdown pass. The 49ers won the game 38-16. Even though the Dolphins came up short, Marino did not. He set Super Bowl marks with 29 completions and 50 attempts.

1986 Super Bowl XX: Bears on a Romp

Two first-time Super Bowl teams met to play Super Bowl XX. They were the Chicago Bears and the New England Patriots. The Chicago Bears, coached by Mike Ditka, were on the prowl for a victory. They had shut out both teams they faced in the playoffs. The Bears didn't skunk the Patriots in the Super Bowl, but they won by the widest margin in Super Bowl history.

New England had the lead when Tony Franklin kicked a field goal in the first period. It didn't last long. Kevin Butler came back with two in a row for the Bears. The Bears were on a roll. Matt Suhey added a touchdown on an 11-yard run before the period ended. Jim McMahon made another touchdown and Butler added another field goal before the half. In the third quarter, McMahon scored another touchdown. Then Reggie Phillips intercepted a Steve Grogan pass and ran it back 28 yards for a touchdown. The Bears had the Super Bowl's biggest fullback ever, William "Refrigerator" Perry. The 235-pound Perry added a cherry to the sundae. The Fridge bulled in from the one-yard line for Chicago's fifth touchdown of the day. Henry Waechter tackled Grogan in the end zone for a safety and the Bears won 46-10.

Jim McMahon scores a touchdown.

1987 Super Bowl XXI: One for the Giants

In 1987 the New York Giants won their first NFL championship in 30 years. The trip to the Super Bowl was their first. The Giants were pitted against the explosive Denver Broncos. The game was played on January 25, 1987, at the Rose Bowl in Pasadena, California. The Giants were solid favorites because of their defense. Phil Simms was the Giants quarterback. Simms and the offense had always been second fiddle to the Giants defense, who got most of the publicity. Simms was good, but no one expected him to have a record-breaking day. He put on perhaps the greatest show of any quarterback in Super Bowl history.

The Bronco's John Elway was the dominant quarterback in the first half. The Broncos led 10-9 at halftime. Then Simms went to work and became the Giants main man. He also became a Super Bowl record breaker. In the second half of the game alone, he made ten straight completions, setting a new Super Bowl record. Simms completed a record-breaking 22 of 25 passes, gaining 268 yards. Ten of his passes were for first downs. Three others were for touchdowns. His 88 percent completion accuracy set another record. Simms broke the 73.5 percent record set by Cincinnati's Ken Anderson in the 1982 Super Bowl.

The Broncos got a touchdown with about three minutes left. Denver's John Elway tossed a 53-yarder to Vance Johnson, but the game was already out of reach. The Giants won 39-20 for the Super Bowl title. Phil Simms was the unanimous choice as the game's Most Valuable Player.

A Super Performance

Super Bowl records didn't compare with regular season game records, which had been set over seven decades. But that changed in Super Bowl XXI. Phil Simms outperformed every quarterback in Super Bowl history! The 30-year-old quarterback had completed 22 of 25 passes. That was 88 percent of his attempts. A closer look at the record book makes Simms's performance even more outstanding. In the history of professional football, only two passers who threw a minimum 20 in a game had a better one-game percentage. One was Ken Anderson of the Cincinnati Bengals. Ken had a 90.91 percentage in a 1974 game. Lynn Dickey of the Green Bay Packers had a 90.48 percentage for a 1981 game.

The Gatorade Bath

A lot of Super Bowl activity happens on the sidelines. At the 1987 Super Bowl, the TV cameras were told to keep an eye on the Giants' Harry Carson in the fourth quarter. Harry controlled the Gatorade. He had been dumping it on Coach Bill Parcells all season, when the Giants won. It became a national curiosity. Millions of television viewers waited and watched. Here came Carson again, wearing a yellow jacket as camouflage. He snuck up behind Parcells. He lifted the bucket. Splash! He gave Parcells another orange victory bath!

The shower

1988 Super Bowl XXII: Denver Broncos vs. Washington Redskins—Redskins Upset Broncos

The Denver Broncos met the Washington Redskins at San Diego's Jack Murphy Stadium for Super Bowl XXII. In the minds of many, the difference in this Super Bowl came down to two things. They were the superior ability of John Elway compared to the average ability of Doug Williams. The Bronco's Elway was called one of the most dangerous quarterbacks in football. The Redskins' Williams heard more questions about his being the first black quarterback to start a Super Bowl game than about the game itself.

Sports analysts said stopping John Elway was the biggest key to the game. At first, it looked like they were right. It was still early in the first quarter when the Broncos had a 10-0 lead. Then Williams had to leave the game with an injured leg. He came back, his knee wrapped. At the same time, Elway's blistering start had slowed.

A wild second quarter upset all the pre-game predictions. In less than 15 minutes, Washington had an incredible 35-10 advantage. It took a record-setting performance by Doug Williams to do it. The Skins set a postseason record of five touchdowns in a period. They had compiled an amazing 356 yards in total offense. Williams was 9 for 11 in the period, good for 228 yards and four touchdowns. Nothing like this blitz had been seen before. The Broncos could not get going again. Washington coasted home for one of the easiest Super Bowl wins ever, 42-10.

Doug Williams was named the Most Valuable Player. He completed 18 passes in 29 tries for a record 340 yards and four scores. Ricky Sanders also set a Super Bowl mark with

Doug Williams, Most Valuable Player

193 receiving yards. Rookie Timmy Smith set a new rushing mark with 204 yards on 22 carries. As a team, the Skins went into the record books with 602 total yards.

What about John Elway? He was supposed to dominate the game. Elway just didn't have it. He was 14 for 38 in passing. He got 257 yards and one score. He had three tosses intercepted and seven deflected. He was sacked by the Redskin defense five times.

1989 Super Bowl XXIII: Comeback for the Niners

On January 22, 1989, the San Francisco 49ers met the Cincinnati Bengals in Super Bowl XXIII. The game took place at Miami's Joe Robbie Stadium before 75,000 fans. Over 100 million more watched on TV. This Super Bowl was a close contest. Finally, only three minutes were left in the game. Cincinnati was ahead 16-13. The ball was on San Francisco's eight-yard line. Then the 49ers made a comeback. The 49ers' Joe Montana completed eight of nine passes. His final drive was one for the ages. He guided his team nearly the length of the field. With 34 seconds left, he found John Taylor in the end zone for a 10-yard strike. The crowd gasped, then roared. Touchdown! San Francisco won, 20-16.

Lucky Charms

Jerry Rice, the 49ers' wide receiver, had a superstition. He always wore a white towel hanging from his uniform pants for luck. Jerry was named Most Valuable Player of Super Bowl XXIII. Wearing his towel, he caught 11 passes for 215 yards (a Super Bowl record) and one touchdown.

The 1989 Super Bowl was Joe Montana's first time back to the Big Game in four years. Joe's wife gave him a surprise for luck. She packed the jersey Joe had worn during Super Bowl XIX. That game was his showdown with Dan Marino and the Miami Dolphins. With the jersey was a note: "Last time you wore this, you did pretty well. Maybe you want to wear it again." When the game began, Joe was back in his old jersey. And back to his old form! He engineered the most dramatic finish in Super Bowl history. And he did it in a used jersey!

1990 Super Bowl XXIV: Broncos Busting 49ers

The San Francisco 49ers were back. They met the Denver Broncos in Super Bowl XXIV. The scene was the Louisiana Superdome in New Orleans on January 28, 1990. Montana and his teammates made sure there would be no need for a comeback effort this time. Jerry Rice's hands helped him set another Super Bowl. He caught seven passes for 148 yards and a Super Bowl record—three touchdowns. The 49ers' Joe Montana threw a record five-touchdown passes and won the Most Valuable Player Award for the third time. The 49ers demolished the Broncos, 55-10.

1991 Super Bowl XXV: The Giants' Great Escape

Super Bowl XXV was the closest in history. And this thriller wasn't decided until the last four seconds of the game. The Buffalo Bills faced the New York Giants. The Bills were in the downtrodden AFC. The AFC had not won a Super Bowl since the Raiders beat the Redskins 38-9 in Super Bowl XVIII. In the last six Super Bowls, the NFC outscored the AFC 240-86. The Bills had never played in a Super Bowl. But the Bills and their no-huddle offense had scored a whopping 95 points in two games before the Super Bowl. The Giants had just defeated the two-time defending Super Bowl champion 49ers in San Francisco. Yet the Giants were seven point underdogs. They'd been called predictable and conservative. But they were powerful. They out-conditioned almost every team. They didn't make many mistakes. They won many games in the fourth quarter. And they did it again in Super Bowl XXV.

The Bills were hanging on to a 19-17 lead. Then the Giants made a 74-yard drive. It set up Matt Bahr's game-winning 21-yard field goal, kicked with 7:20 remaining. Unfortunately for the Bills, Scott Norwood missed a 47-yard field goal with four seconds left to play. It clinched the championship for the Giants. The Giants beat the Bills 20-19 in the closest and most dramatic Super Bowl ever.

The Giants beat the clock.

Ottis Anderson: 1991 MVP

The last time Ottis Anderson played in a Super Bowl, he carried the ball two times for one yard. It was a one-yard touchdown in the New York Giants' 39-20 win over Denver in Super Bowl XXI. He was a backup to the Giants' Joe Morris. Morris carried 20 times for 67 yards in the title game. So while Anderson received a Super Bowl ring, he said he did not feel he earned it. Ottis said a long time ago: "If I got to play in another Super Bowl, I'd be a most valuable player." Ottis got another chance, and he *was* the game's MVP.

At the Super Bowl Ottis Anderson, age 34, was the oldest running back in the NFL. It didn't slow him down. He rushed for 102 yards on 21 carries. He gained 63 of those yards on 14 carries in the second half. His biggest moment came in the third quarter. He made a 75-yard scoring drive, the biggest drive of the Giants' season. Anderson scored from one yard out, standing up. It was the touchdown that put the Giants ahead 17-12. The drive lasted nine minutes, 29 seconds, a record for possession time on a touchdown drive.

M.I.P.? (Most Interesting Player)

The Buffalo Bills' linebacker Ray Bentley might be the most interesting player at the Super Bowl. He was a standout player. He was also the author of several children's books featuring "Darby the Dinosaur." The Bills backup offensive lineman Mitch Frerotte said: "He's a killer football player and he writes *children's* books?"

Bentley paints as well as writes. He was in the habit, along with Frerotte, of painting his face before games. He explains: "I started doing it in high school in 1978. We had a game on

Halloween and I was a big Alice Cooper fan. There happened to be some watercolor paints there. I put it on in the other room where the team was and they just went crazy. We just killed the other team we played that night, and it was a big inspiration for us, so I've been doing it ever since."

Hard-Nosed Guy

Two goalposts were set up 50 feet apart on Main Street in Hornell, N. Y., a few days after Super Bowl XXV. Why? About 1,000 Buffalo Bills fans came to see Rob Roberts pay his debt. Roberts was a sportswriter for the *Hornell Evening Tribune*. In September Roberts wrote: "I like the Bills as much as anybody, but I've gotta be realistic. This is not a Super Bowl team, folks. In fact, if these guys get to the Super Bowl, I'll push a peanut down Main Street with my nose."

Said Roberts: "I really didn't scrape (my nose) too bad."

Best of Games, Worst of Times

Super Bowl XXV was unlike any other Super Bowl. It was the closest Super Bowl in history. It was the game's 25-year silver anniversary. And it took place in tense times. Americans were thinking about the war in the Persian Gulf. The NFL talked about changing the date of the game due to war in the Middle East. Closed-circuit television sets were ready to switch to war news if necessary. Oversized scoreboards could show war news. Extra time was allowed between quarters to allow ABC to give longer news updates. Security was tight to prevent any terrorist attacks. Fans waved tiny American flags. And just before the kickoff, a flight of F-16 fighter planes roared across the sky. It was both a show of patriotism and a put-down to Iraq's leader Saddam Hussein.

The halftime show was called "A Small World Salute to 25 Years of the Super Bowl." The show was produced by Walt Disney World. It featured 2,000 children from the Tampa Bay area. They were dressed as miniature football players, cheerleaders, and referees. The halftime show was interrupted for an update on the Gulf war. But the game went on without trouble.

Meanwhile, the half-million American troops watched the Super Bowl on outdoor screens in Saudi Arabia. At the same time, they were on alert in case of a missile attack. The game passed without a Scud launch. The U.S. troops enjoyed a game that many back home had urged be canceled because of the war.

Golden Oldie

Pop singer Whitney Houston sang "The Star Spangled Banner" before the Super Bowl game in 1991. People liked the way she sang it so much that they asked for recordings. Whitney made a cassette single and a video. The profits from the sales were to go to a charity in the war effort selected by Houston.

Super Bowl Records Set in 1991

The Giants set records for the longest time of possession in a Super Bowl (40:33). Their time topped San Francisco's mark of 39:31 from Super Bowl XXIV. The Giants set a record for longest time of possession on a touchdown drive (9:19). They also set a record for the closest winning margin (1 point). Both teams set a record for fewest turnovers (none) in a Super Bowl.

Super Bowl XXVI: Inside the Dome

There were now 363 days until Super Bowl XXVI. The game would be played January 26, 1992, at the Metrodome in Minneapolis. It would be the second Super Bowl in a January cold-weather climate. Domed stadiums, like the Metrodome, offer ideal playing conditions. No wet or frozen fields, no fog, no rainouts. Not even a blizzard could stop the Super Bowl now!

Super Bowl XXVII

Phoenix, Arizona, was the city chosen for the 1993 Super Bowl. But the NFL threatened to move the Super Bowl to a city in another state. Why? Arizona voters rejected a state holiday honoring Martin Luther King, Jr., Day. Only three U.S. states— New Hampshire, Montana, and Arizona—do not officially observe the holiday. Nearly half of the football players in the NFL are African-Americans. Many players say they don't want to play in a state that refuses to honor slain civil rights leader, Dr. Martin Luther King. Many people in Arizona were dismayed by the results of the vote. Some legislators have vowed to add the holiday without the voters' approval. But people who don't want the holiday observed have said they will fight such a move. Phoenix would lose more than $200 million in ticket sales and tourist business if the Super Bowl is moved.

Super Bowl Timelines

1966: The new AFL and the old NFL agreed to merge.

1967: Packers reserve receiver Max McGee was the star of Super Bowl I. After having caught 4 passes all year for the Packers, McGee replaced the injured Boyd Dowler early in the game. He caught seven passes for 138 yards and two touchdowns. The Green Bay Packers beat the Kansas City Chiefs.

1968: Packers coach Vince Lombardi got a standing ovation from the 15 NFL owners at a board meeting the day after his Packers won Super Bowl II.

1969: Joe Namath of the New York Jets was named MVP of Super Bowl III for his leadership as well as his quarterbacking.

1971: The Super Bowl was won by a field goal in the final seconds. Rookie Jim O'Brien kicked for the Colts. He was so nervous, he tried pulling up blades of grass to check the wind. Someone reminded him they were playing on artificial turf!

1971: The only MVP from a losing team was Chuck Howley of the Dallas Cowboys. It was the only time in Super Bowl history that the MVP was from the losing team.

1973: The Miami Dolphins won Super Bowl VII, capping a 17-0 year, the only perfect season in NFL history.

1975: The Steel Curtain Defense became one of the four teams that fell on Minnesota. The Vikings finished with only 17 yards rushing.

1975: Pittsburgh's Franco Harris was named MVP when he rushed for 158 yards on 34 carries. He was the all-time leading rusher in Super Bowl history and scored four touchdowns in the Steelers' four Super Bowl victories.

1976: Terry Bradshaw never saw the 64-yard touchdown pass he threw to Lynn Swann in Super Bowl X. He was knocked unconscious during the play.

1976: The Seattle Seahawks became a member of the NFC's Western Division. The Tampa Bay Buccaneers joined the Western Division of the AFC.

1977: Seattle and Tampa switched conferences. Tampa Bay was now in the NFC Central Division. Seattle was in the AFC Western Division.

1977: The Minnesota Vikings lost the Super Bowl for the fourth time in the decade. They were defeated by the Chiefs, Dolphins, Steelers, and Raiders. Carl Eller, standout Vikings defensive end, played in all four defeats. He said: "People just remember the winners. They forget how hard it is to get there."

1980: Pittsburgh Steelers quarterback Terry Bradshaw played in the last of his four Super Bowl games. He had earned two MVP awards: 1979 and 1980.

1981: The coach of the Super Bowl's Cincinnati Bengals, Forrest Gregg, had played for the Green Bay Packers in Super Bowl I and II.

1982: Five of the ten highest-rated telecasts of all time have been Super Bowls. Super Bowl XVI, the 49ers vs. the Bengals, was the top-rated of all.

1982: Only nine regular season games were played due to a football strike.

1986: Nearly 62 percent of America's 245 million people watched the Chicago Bears rout the New England Patriots in the Super Bowl.

1989: The 49ers' Charles Haley had six tackles and two sacks in Super Bowl XXIII as San Francisco's defense did not allow a touchdown.

1989: Although he has won three MVP awards and has guided San Francisco to four titles, Joe Montana is remembered best for driving the 49ers 92 yards for the winning touchdown in the closing seconds of XXIII.

1991: Super Bowl XXV, played in Tampa, was the seventh straight victory for the NFC. The last AFC team to win the Super Bowl was the Los Angeles Raiders in Super Bowl XVIII—the only other Super Bowl to be held in Tampa.

1991: Ottis Anderson was only the fifth back in 25 Super Bowls to win the MVP award. He was the first to win the Pete Rozelle Trophy, as the award is now called.

Index